IMAGES
of America

ALONG THE BALTIMORE & OHIO RAILROAD

FROM CUMBERLAND TO UNIONTOWN

IMAGES
of America

ALONG THE BALTIMORE & OHIO RAILROAD

FROM CUMBERLAND TO UNIONTOWN

Marci Lynn McGuinness

ARCADIA

Published by Arcadia Publishing,
an imprint of Tempus Publishing, Inc.
2 Cumberland Street
Charleston, SC 29401

Printed in Great Britain.

Library of Congress Catalog Card Number: 98-87774

For all general information contact Arcadia Publishing at:
Telephone 843-853-2070
Fax 843-853-0044
E-Mail arcadia@charleston.net

For customer service and orders:
Toll-Free 1-888-313-BOOK

Visit us on the internet at http://www.arcadiaimages.com

This book is dedicated to William Love,
a carpenter foreman for the Baltimore & Ohio Railroad
during the time these photographs were taken in 1890–1891.
I thank his descendants for their contribution of the book
Baltimore & Ohio Railroad Views of Bridges and Buildings,
Pittsburgh Division, From Cumberland to Pittsburgh and Branches, 1891.
A special thanks to Lori Rittenhouse, Dave Glisan, Charlotte Fosbrink,
Edith Holt, Debbie and Mike Konechny, and Linn Newman
for their generous loan of photographs.
It is to the credit of interested people like these
that we continue to preserve local history.

CONTENTS

INTRODUCTION

This is the first volume of a two-volume set called *Along the Baltimore & Ohio Railroad From Cumberland to Uniontown* and *Along the Baltimore & Ohio Railroad From Connellsville to Pittsburgh.* As mentioned on p. 4, a book called *Baltimore & Ohio Railroad Views of Bridges and Buildings, Pittsburgh Division, From Cumberland to Pittsburgh and Branches, 1891* was the inspiration for these volumes. The old publication is a compilation of over 200 photographs taken by photographers hired by the railroad.

In my research, I have discovered that a famous photographer named William Henry Jackson is responsible for these photographs and photographs of various railroad lines at the time. Jackson's work includes his round-the-world expedition for the World Transportation Commission during which he photographed railroads and many other forms of transportation in 24 countries from 1894 to 1896.

From 1870 to 1878, Jackson photographed the Rocky Mountains for Francis V. Hayden's *Geological and Geographic Survey of the Territories.* Much to Jackson's credit, he focused on what became Yellowstone National Park.

The Baltimore & Ohio Railroad was incorporated in 1826 by the legislature of Maryland. Charles Carroll laid its first stone on July 4, 1828. At the historical ceremony, Carroll remarked, "I consider this one of the most important acts of my life, second only to my signing of the Declaration of Independence, even if it be second to that."

This first rail line extended from Baltimore to Ellicott's Mills, a mere 13 miles. On May 22, 1830, this line, with rail cars pulled by horses and mules, was opened to passengers. In the first four months of passenger service, the company took in $20,012.36.

The Baltimore & Ohio Railroad was the first railroad of any length in this country to offer passenger and freight service between stations that were separated by many miles. The B&O can also take the honor for using the first locomotive built in the United

States. Constructed by Peter Cooper, the locomotive was first used on August 28, 1830. It had a small engine with a single cylinder about 3.5 inches in diameter; these engines were placed on wheels which were 30 inches wide. The trains traveled at a speed of approximately 5 to 18 miles per hour, and the 13-mile ride from Baltimore to Ellicott's Mills took 57 minutes with 30 people on board. The locomotive was fueled by anthracite coal with a fan making a draft through the fire box in the bottom of a boiler.

On December 1, 1831, a 61-mile line opened to Frederick, Maryland. On April 1, 1832, another 69 miles were added to Point of Rocks. A 32-mile line opened to Bladensburg on July 20, 1834. Washington was reached by a 40-mile line on August 25, 1834. Harper's Ferry celebrated their new 81-mile track on December 1, 1834. On June 1, 1842, a person could travel 123 miles to Hancock. That same year, on November 5, the line grew to 178 miles reaching Cumberland. Two hundred and six miles to Peidmont opened on July 21, 1851. The 302 miles to Fairmont, West Virginia, opened on June 22, 1853, and, on the first of that year, the B&O reached Wheeling.

Cities, villages, and towns prospered as transportation improved. Coal and lumber were hauled from the country to the areas of large population. Citizens traveled as never before.

John W. Garrett, president of the Baltimore & Ohio Railroad, was a hands-on executive. He saw to the smallest of details and ran his rail with a proverbial iron fist. It was his fierce dedication that took the B&O from being a tiny local railway to a giant in American transportation.

The railroad in this book travels from Cumberland, Maryland, to Uniontown, Pennsylvania. This section is of particular interest because, here, the railroad was in direct competition with the famed National Road. During the early years of the B&O, the National Road from Cumberland to Wheeling was the gateway to the West. Stage coaches, herds of farm animals, wagoners, and the like filled the long dirt pike. Taverns, inns, and stables lined the road, servicing travelers. Life was good when the railroad built its line along the Youghiogheny River.

In 1835, the first surveys were made by the B&O from here through Fayette County, Pennsylvania. George Washington had suggested the path go through the mountains along the Youghiogheny River. They all began at the confluence of the Youghiogheny and Casselman Rivers along the left bank of the Yough to New Haven (Connellsville's west side). From here, the routes varied along streams called Boland's Run, Opossum Run, and Bull's Run to Redstone Creek and onward to the Monongahela River. Another route came down along Coal and Shutes Run to its confluence with Redstone Creek and continued on to the mouth of the Redstone. By 1838, the B&O was running low on funds after completing the line from Baltimore to Cumberland, and the Pennsylvania plans were put on hold. This delay exceeded the time allowed under the act of assembly, and those who favored the B&O coming through southwestern Pennsylvania were now favoring the Pennsylvania Railroad Company. The National Road was also a strong competitor with growing railroads. There were those who fought against the great steel locomotives.

On November 25 and 26, 1835, a convention of delegates from Baltimore, Cumberland, Pittsburgh, Wheeling, and Uniontown met at the Episcopal church in

Brownsville, Pennsylvania. Congressman Andrew Stewart was elected president of the assembly. Here they agreed to enlist the help of all municipalities along the proposed B&O Railroad through southwestern Pennsylvania. Commercial and social demands to move products from the east to the west pushed our country's leaders to fight for the completion of the great railway.

In 1844, the Monongahela Slack Water Navigation Company began business, and the National Road now had an ally in its fight to squash the railway that threatened its importance. Former-Congressman Henry W. Beeson had been an advocate of the railroad but spoke against its completion in July 1845. When the Pennsylvania Legislature refused to renew B&O's charter, B&O built through Virginia, skirting the southwest corner of Pennsylvania to Wheeling. This line opened in 1852 and instantly halted travel on the National Road. Then, B&O bought a line which was already built to Pittsburgh. The Pennsylvania Railroad, which came from the east to Pittsburgh, reached Connellsville in 1855 after that town pledged itself as collateral in order to pay for its connection. Andrew Stewart fought to get the railroad built from Connellsville through Ohiopyle and on to Cumberland. This was finished in 1871, one year before his death.

The Baltimore & Ohio Railroad leased this line from the Pennsylvania Railroad and then bought it, realizing their goal of a road over the mountains following the Youghiogheny. The Fayette County Railroad Company was formed by Uniontown officials to connect the county seat with Connellsville. By 1860, they fulfilled this dream with a station at the corner of East Penn and North Beeson. Four years later, the Pittsburgh and Connellsville line leased this branch. The B&O then bought it and constructed a station on North Gallatin Avenue in Uniontown.

As Fayette County moved into their great coal and coke boom era, the railroads became even more important to commerce. Connellsville's famous soft coal was taken to coke ovens, and the coke shipped to Pittsburgh steel mills. From the mountains surrounding Ohiopyle, lumber was shipped to coal mines.

An upswing in the economy prompted the creation of passenger trains. Ohiopyle saw its first tourist boom when travelers could come enjoy the beauty of the falls and river for just $1 round trip from Pittsburgh or Cumberland. Hotels were built by Andrew Stewart and his sons along the Youghioghony's wild water. There was plenty of work for the average man, and Uniontown was filled with millionaires. Prosperity reined until the Depression, when lumber mills and coal mines became ghost yards. The invention of the automobile hurt passenger train travel, and the great railways slowed their pace for hard times. This book covers a time of great economy and growth in Maryland and southwestern Pennsylvania.

One

FROM CUMBERLAND TO GLENCOE

The Narrows, East of Frostburg, Md.

Wills Creek cuts through Haystack and Wills Mountains just west of Cumberland, Maryland, forming a gap called "The Narrows." At the west end of the Narrows, Braddock Run joins Wills Creek to Eckhart Mines. The B&O Railroad turned right at Wills Creek, passing where Jennings Run flows into Wills Creek.

In the 1870s, the Baltimore & Ohio Railroad's John W. Garrett built this landmark, the Baltimore & Ohio Hotel & Station, in Cumberland, Maryland.

This is an 1870s photograph of the old Rolling Mill in Cumberland, Maryland. Before the steel rail, this mill was an important part of the B&O operations.

This March 30, 1909 picture shows Lover's Leap in Cumberland, Maryland.

This bird's-eye view of Cumberland, Maryland, was taken on January 31, 1897.

This photograph offers a view, looking west, of Baltimore Street in Cumberland, Maryland, on September 18, 1908.

Riverside Park is pictured here on January 30, 1916.

Mount Savage Junction is seen here in 1890 from the east. The track to the right was a small 54-car side track.

In 1890, this plate-girder bridge was a new type of construction. It was built over Jennings Run just west of Mount Savage Junction. This was Bridge Number 1 on the P&C (B&O).

Juanita Coke Works is seen here in 1890. During the great coal and coke boom, beehive ovens lined Maryland and southwestern Pennsylvania. It was here the coal was cooked and turned to coke. The coke would then be shipped by railway to the steel mills of Pittsburgh.

Pictured here in 1890, this was Bridge Number 3 at Ellerslie, Maryland, just south of the Keystone State's border. Bridge Number 3 was the shortest on the line. It served as a cattle pass through the 1960s. Ellerslie had an interchange yard that was small but vital.

This is bridge Number 7 over Gladdens Creek in 1890. The two-car train on the left is the team that traveled along the B&O and took many of the photographs in this book today. Just ten years later, the quaint structure was replaced by a plate-girder model.

On the west side of Cooks Mills over Wills Creek sat this four-span through truss, pictured here in 1890. Notice that part of the bridge is built over land. You will see this in many of these bridges as fill was not available then. This structure was replaced with a plate-girder bridge whose approach was over fill.

Cooks Mills Station in 1890 was a bustling little town. The side track here was replaced in 1912 by a narrow gauge railroad. It was called High, Dry, and Windy (HD&W). The Cooks Mills Coal and Clay Company was opened but closed its doors during the Depression. Cooks Mills lies just 2.5 miles north of the cattle pass, across the Pennsylvania line.

This photograph is of the Hyndman Bridge Number 8 in 1890. Mr. E.K. Hyndman was the general superintendent of the P&C when the line was built to Cumberland.

Hyndman Bridge Number 9 is seen here in 1890.

Hyndman Bridge Number 10 is seen here in 1890.

Hyndman Bridge Number 11 is seen here in 1890.

Pictured here is the Hyndman Station in 1890. To the far left you can see an early electric power plant with an engine garage to its rear. This railroad station was constructed in 1883. There were two stations here—one belonged to the P&C and the other was owned by the PRR.

Bridge Number 12, about 2 miles west of Hyndman at Gooseberry Run, is seen here in 1890. Later, the village on the curve (Gooseberry) changed its name to Hobitzel.

This is the town of Williams in 1890. It lies one mile down the line from Bracken Curve. Fire brick was made here, and a few clay mines have been located. Williams had a telegraph office until 1920 with "W" as their call letter.

Fairhope's west end is pictured here in 1890. The B&O is to the right, and to the left lie two side tracks. It is believed that the building to the left is the telegraph office that served Fairhope until 1898.

This 1890 picture shows Falls Cut Bridge Number 13. Just a mile west of Fairhope, Wills Creek joins Bush Creek after doing a 180-degree turn around a mountainous knob. Falls Cut Bridge 13 was the first bridge to cross Wills Creek from the west side.

Bridge Number 14 was the second to cross Wills Creek and was built in 1871. This 1890 photo shows a man standing on the bridge. Is it photographer William Henry Jackson? We may never know.

Glencoe was a station which provided water to the steam engines. This country village was a mile west of Southampton and had a side track for 61 cars. A telegraph office served residents there until a third track was constructed in 1911. In 1901, about 2.5 miles west of Glencoe, a 16-lever Standard A interlocker operated in a tower from 1901 to 1935 with the call letters "HN."

Two

SANDPATCH, MEYERSDALE, MARKLETON, SALISBURY, AND BERLIN

Beck's Cut is pictured here in 1890.

Bridge Number 15 going into Beck's Cut is seen here. Some of the photography crew poses for a photograph on a lovely day in 1890.

This 1890 picture shows Bridge Number 16 at Beck's Cut.

Fall's Cut Bridge Number 17 is seen here in 1890. The west end of Fall's Cut took 300,000 feet of oak lumber to build and had braces towering as high as 75 feet above the water. Annual repairs were required which became costly. Around 1900, the Fall's Cut Tunnel was developed. The man standing by the Fall's Cut sign on the bridge is Supervisor M. Foley, who had an interlocker nearby named after him.

Bridge Number 18 at Fall's Cut crosses Wills Creek to the east of the knob. The Bollman Truss-style bridge was designed and patented by Master of Road Wendell Bollman. This iron icon was one of the earliest spans. Bollman had a factory in Canton, Maryland, where the parts for the bridge were built.

Sand Patch Station is pictured here in 1890. This village once sat over the tunnels but moved closer to the area of the station, making the town a center of commerce. A sandy patch of ground lies close to the station along the road, and residents named the town after that sand patch. A mountain spring filled the water tower, built in 1885. Two more towers and a dam were built to store the water. Sand Patch is 2,258 feet above sea level, making it the highest point in Pennsylvania for the B&O.

Bridge Number 19 over Flaugherty Creek, seen here in 1890, is at the Eastern Continental Divide. This stream ran both east and west, forming a cleft in the Allegheny Mountains. The B&O came into Flaugherty Gap from the southeast and made a hard right to climb the Sand Patch Summit.

This wooden truss crossed Flaugherty along a rough spot in the creek where it took tons of rock to support the short structure.

This 1890 picture shows Bridge Number 24 over Flaugherty Creek as it runs through the rough gap west of Sand Patch.

Bridge Number 25 was the last in the gap taking you into Sand Patch. Some of the photography crew can be seen on the bridge here in 1890.

This tunnel was necessary east of Sand Patch and was built on a one percent grade. Sand Patch was at the height of its popularity at the turn of the century. A 6-lever interlocker served here from 1899 until a 32-lever interlocker replaced it in 1904.

Just a mile west of Sand Patch, the Keystone Station held a telegraph office. The grade of decline on this side of Sand Patch was much more modest, holding valuable coal underneath its surface.

Meyersdale was the major bustling town west of Sand Patch. Many townsfolk came to the fancy station this day to pose for the camera. Flaugherty Creek meets the Casselman River here.

Bridge Number 26 at Meyersdale crosses a gap high above the railroad tracks. Meyersdale was once known as Meyers Mill. It was not as busy as the Salisbury Station next on the line.

Salisbury Junction holds the honor of having the first branch line this side of Cumberland, Maryland. Even before the main line opened here in 1871, many more branches sprung up. This 1890 photo barely shows the 40-car side track to the right.

Notice the man leaning over the front side of the Salisbury Junction Bridge, shown here in 1890.

West Salisbury Branch Station is pictured here in 1890. This line ran upstream through the Casselman Valley for 12 miles to Niverton, surrounded by the Negro and Meadow Mountains. Many side tracks were formed as lumber mills and coal mines prospered here.

Bridge Number 27 at Blue Curve is seen here in 1890.

This 1890 photograph shows Bridge Number 28 at Yoder. Yoder was 2 miles east of Garrett and served as a "helper" station, supplying coal and water.

This is a picture of the bridge at Blue Curve in 1890. Men in their suits and black hats pose on a very short straight wooden number.

Garrett Station, pictured here in 1890, was just 4 miles west of Salisbury Station. It was named for John Garrett, president of the B&O. Here a tower (not seen) served as the only interlocker from Sand Patch to Rockwood. The Berlin Branch began here.

Garrett Bridge crossing the Casselman River is seen here in 1890.

Weaver Run Bridge in Garrett is shown here in 1890.

Bridge Number 600 was the start of the 8-mile branch to Berlin. Notice the station to the left and the group of children to the right on the tracks. This line served many mines along Buffalo Creek.

Bridge Number 601 crossed Buffalo Creek just 1.5 miles outside Garrett. The rough, timber-and-post bridge had a walkway to the left where two men stand.

Bridge 602 along the Berlin Branch crossed Buffalo Creek.

The Salisbury Branch Bridge crossed the Casselman River about a mile from Salisbury Junction. This fancy Howe Timber Truss Bridge was replaced by a steel through truss bridge in 1897.

The bridges on this page and on the following three pages all served the Salisbury Branch for many years.

Three

ROCKWOOD, SOMERSET, AND JOHNSTOWN

The Rockwood Station shown here was enlarged in 1882. It was an important station with water storage. The Somerset and Cambria Branch ran from Rockwood to Johnstown. The line to Connellsville began here on the right.

The first bridge leaving Rockwood crossed Coxes Creek, which ran along the line to Somerset. Rockwood lies 1,814 feet above sea level.

Bridge Number 202 over Coxes Creek is shown here in 1890.

In this picture of Bridge Number 203 across Coxes Creek, notice that the stone walls hold much of the bridge. The portion of the bridge that actually crosses the water is quite short.

Bridge Number 204 over Coxes Creek, pictured here in 1890, is just this side of Somerset.

This is an 1890 picture of Keslers Bridge.

The Somerset Station was built in the mid-1880s as part of the Somerset and Cambria Branch. A "loop" was constructed from Somerset to Quemahoning Junction, passing through Boswell at its uppermost point. In this photo, the 11-car train and caboose is heading north. Just behind the train sat a large coal dock.

Somerset's courthouse and the soldier monument on Main Street are seen in this picture taken on June 5, 1918. This impressive courthouse building still serves the quaint town today.

This September 8, 1919 picture shows the County Trust Company in Somerset. Community members gather in this bustling town during the coal and coke boom of southwestern Pennsylvania.

The Main Street of Somerset is seen here on August 11, 1916. At this time, early automobiles joined the horse and buggy in small towns all over America.

A trestle bridge just west of Somerset is in this 1890 photograph. Later, a deck plate-girder bridge was built here. Notice the tall building in the background—an old-fashioned skyscraper?

Bridge Number 207 leaving Somerset is pictured here in 1890. The B&O kept many sawmills in business during this time.

Bridge Number 208, pictured here in 1890, is the next along the Somerset and Cambria Branch.

I wish I could tell you who the men are in this 1890 picture, but my research has not come up with the facts. Dapper though, aren't they?

The little town of Boswell, pictured here in 1890, was on the Somerset and Cambria Branch. Just a mile outside of Somerset on this line the elevation rose to 2,128 feet above sea level. This quaint scene features fresh wash on the clothesline.

This small wooden bridge allowed the B&O to continue to Quemahoning over a tiny still stream.

Bridge Number 213 in this 1890 photo shows two men taking a break. I wonder if they wrote the message on the top left plank stating, "Go to C.F. Morrow The Photographer." This is a typical flat wooden bridge braced by stone and earth.

This next bridge, pictured in 1890, boasts a steel-girder system.

All is quiet on the tracks in 1890.

Bridge Number 217 is shown here in 1890.

This bridge seems rather long to be without a stone pillar in the center. The picture is dated 1890.

You can see the center pillar sturdying Bridge Number 223's low-lying structure in this 1890 picture.

Bridge Number 228 is a double steel structure allowing the B&O to cross Stony Creek. This picture is dated 1890.

This 1890 photograph shows another long steel bridge crossing Stony Creek.

Bridge Number 234 was a short one and is pictured here in 1890.

Bridge Number 238 is pictured here in 1890 with stone walls below and a short horizontal pass.

This close-up photograph shows the rough terrain on which workers had to build the numerous bridges. Southwestern Pennsylvania is an area with many streams.

Seen in this 1890 photo, Stoney Creek is a wide and low body of water in Hollsopple.

Bridge Number 250 is just one in a line of many bridges. This picture is 1890.

Kaufman Run runs into Stoney Creek about 2 miles north of Hollsopple. Here is shown the water jug that Kaufman Run supplied. This area was being timbered, as is apparent in this 1890 picture, and there was a three-car company side track here for that purpose.

Here is a scene along Stoney Creek in 1890.

A single-tiered steel bridge crosses Paint Creek in this 1890 photo.

Coal tipples were scattered throughout the region during the great coal and coke boom. Cars filled with coal traveled from mines on side tracks which lead to the mainline of the B&O. There, they would fill the large coal cars. This is an 1890 picture.

Just north of a town called Krings, the Hog Back Tunnel pierced the mountain and allowed the B&O to enter Johnstown. The bridge in the foreground is Number 261. The 322-foot tunnel was bored in 1881. It is lined with stone and brick and makes a 9-degree curve from this southern portal, pictured here in 1890.

The 145-foot long South Penn Tunnel was built in 1885 in Geiger on a 3-degree curve. The north portal, shown here in 1890, is built of stone, as are the sidewalls. The roof was made of five-ring brick.

This picture is dated 1890. The summit on the Somerset and Cambria Branch lies at Geiger in the center of the South Penn Tunnel. Geiger sits halfway between Somerset and Friedens.

The Geiger Bridge crosses Stoney Creek as the B&O travels northwest, shown here in 1890.

The B&O went north from Geiger through Quemahoning Junction and Frieden to Stoystown. Notice the incorrect spelling of "Stoyestown." This 1890 photo shows men gathering out front in their vests, hats, and white shirts.

Hooversville was 4 miles down the ridge from Stoystown. This 1890 station had "HV" for its call letters. Notice the general store to the right. Locals pose for the camera along the boardwalk. This station ceased to exist in the mid-1960s.

About 5 miles north of Kaufman Run, the Krings Station stood in good repair in 1890.

The Somerset and Cambria Branch Station in Johnstown, pictured here in 1890, was formerly a school. During the flood of 1889, the water rose to cover the word "station" on the outside sign. Although the sturdy brick structure withstood the water pressure, the old freight house was destroyed and had to be rebuilt. The historic Johnstown flood of 1936 devastated this town and many others downstream. Johnstown was renowned as a great industrial center during the Iron Age.

Four
ROCKWOOD, GLADE RUN, CONFLUENCE, SOMERFIELD, AND FRIENDSVILLE

Bridge Number 34 at Coxes Creek in Rockwood is in this 1890 picture. The creek dumps into the Casselman River in the background here. In earlier days, Rockwood was called Mineral Point.

Bridge Number 35 leaving Rockwood on the Casselman River is the focus of this 1890 photo. It has impressive stone walls for a small crossing. Luckily, riverbeds are a wealth of rock in the mountains here.

This deck plate-girder bridge crosses Middle Creek 3 miles to the west of Rockwood. Stone abutments make a strong base for the photographer's locomotive here. I have a feeling the photographers enjoyed their work on this particular 1890 collection.

Casselman, named after the river, boasted a fine station for such a tiny community. A 60-car sidling served the local area in 1890.

Markleton had a towered station with the tower across the tracks in 1890. Fancy for a small village, don't you think?

The Pinkerton Station in 1890 had a water jug to the west. The 68-car sidling track hauled timber and coal from riverside mills and mines.

An 1890 Ursina Station scene along Laurel Creek can be seen here. The side track served a 19-car train. Another 110-car sidling is not pictured. With coal and coke being king, it is fitting that Coke Oven Hollow is just 2 miles upstream.

One of the first stations in the area was Confluence. The town took its name from the confluence of the Casselman and Youghiogheny Rivers and Laurel Creek. This triple meeting of the waters is also called "Turkey Foot," so named by George Washington in 1754 when he paddled the Youghiogheny and camped here at the onset of the French and Indian War. This picture was taken in 1890.

The B&O telegraph tower in Confluence was destroyed when a 116-car train hit it on May 6, 1987. The freighter derailed and took the life of Robert Leonberger, who had worked for the railroad for 39 years. Toxic chemicals were contained in the 28 derailed cars, resulting in the town's evacuation. The explosion they feared did not happen, much to everyone's relief.

The Methodist church in Confluence, Pennsylvania, is pictured here.

This is an August 30, 1965 shot of Confluence's Baptist church.

This picture was taken on September 12, 1964. The huge hotel and tavern, Dodd's Hotel in Confluence, sits across the road from the tracks and is still in business today.

The road to Confluence in this September 28, 1915 photograph was even more scenic than it is today.

The forests of Fort Hill near Confluence are pictured here in 1910. Palisaded Native-American villages with extensive evidence of housing and burial grounds here date back to early ages.

Is this bridge crossing Laurel Creek?

The Confluence and Oakland Branch is the subject of this 1890 photo.

The photographers continue to pose alongside the picturesque bridges built by B&O carpenter crews.

Bridge Number 703 along the Confluence and Oakland Branch is seen here.

This is a calm river scene along the Youghiogheny in 1890.

Here we see Bridge Number 710 at Buffalo Run heading upstream on the Yough. The line shown here in 1890 passed through Horseshoe Curve, the Tub Run water station, Somerfield, Reason Run, and Buffalo Run before entering Friendsville, Maryland.

Bridge Number 712 crosses the Youghiogheny coming into Friendsville in this 1890 picture. The long wooden structure was not replaced as most of the timber bridges had been. Only two sections became deck plate girders through the years.

Bridge Number 714 is seen here in 1890.

The Somerfield Station served a bustling village along the National Road. This town was covered in water when the Youghiogheny Dam was built by the Army Corp of Engineers from between 1928 and 1939.

The Johnstown flood of 1936 wreaked havoc on towns as far away as Pittsburgh. Here, Somerfield is shown during that famous catastrophe. Shortly after this disaster, Somerfield was closed down and the Yough Dam built to prevent such floods in the future. Today, when droughts occur in the area, you can see the old arched bridge that once reigned there. Some people even find artifacts and coins.

Seen here are ceremonies celebrating the beginning of the surveys for flood control in 1937 at the Youghiogheny House in Somerfield, Pennsylvania.

Daughters of the American Revolution delegates attend the invocation celebration for the Youghiogheny Dam proposal at the Youghiogheny House in Somerfield, Pennsylvania, on April 22, 1937.

Youghiogheney River Bridge, between Cumberland, Md., and Uniontown, Pa., on Hwy. 40

The beautiful scene on Route 40 (the National Road) between Cumberland, Maryland, and Uniontown, Pennsylvania, is the site of the Great Crossing, a point where ancient Native-American trails met. The modern Youghiogheny River Bridge crosses the river at this historical point.

The old Petersburgh Tollhouse in Addison, Pennsylvania, one of six tollhouses along the National Road, was built when the federal government turned the responsibility of the road over to the state in 1835. This structure is built of stone and is run today as a museum. Two others are still in existence. One is in Searights, Pennsylvania, and the other is in LaVale, Maryland.

Selbysport Station is pictured here in 1890.

The Friendsville Station was recently built when this photo was taken in 1890. Half the town showed up for the photo crew. The town was named after a family of Friends who settled here in the early days. The town's telegraph call letters were "GD." Locals called the town "Dodge City" because of all the fights held in the taverns here.

Five

OHIOPYLE, INDIAN CREEK, DUNBAR, AND UNIONTOWN

The Baltimore and Ohio Railroad built this maintenance building in Ohiopyle in 1869. In 1871, the station opened here. This photo was taken in 1875 before the station was replaced with a fancier building. Today, no station stands at this point, but train whistles still fill the air in this quaint mountain village every half hour or so.

This 1891 photograph shows not only the new train station in Ohiopyle, but Tim and Cora Mitchell's 22-room mansion in the background. A sign of the times, the great coal and coke boom brought prosperity to this unique area where the Youghiogheny River's awesome Ohiopyle Falls reign. To the left of the tracks sat the grand Ferncliff Hotel. On the right, travelers could enjoy the Ohiopyle House Hotel. Both were built by Congressman Andrew Stewart and his sons. Stewart fought to bring the railroad here, prompting Ohiopyle's first tourist boom.

This is an 1887 shot of the Ohiopyle Station and gazebo. Thousands came here to enjoy the Youghiogheny River. There were four hotels, several boarding houses, and many rooms to rent in private homes at this time. Notice the covered bridge in the center background and the arched entrance to the left where a long boardwalk took those tourists to the Ferncliff Hotel and to the pavilion and bowling alley along the river's edge.

The Western Maryland Railroad came to Ohiopyle in 1911, building this station on the borough's side of the river. They constructed two long bridges over the Youghiogheny, changing Ferncliff Peninsula forever. This photo depicts the station in the mid-1960s. It still exists as a visitor's center, serving travelers from around the world.

This great gristmill was built by Andrew Stewart's sons after his death in 1872. Andrew came here after retiring from Congress and turning down the position of secretary of the treasury. Instead, Stewart went to the mountains where he built Falls City (Ohiopyle). This mill was used as a saw and planing mill until 1903, when the Kendalls harnessed the Ohiopyle Falls' water power for electricity. During the winter, when the falls froze over, the town's lights would gradually dim until they eventually went out. Folks would argue about whose turn it was to go out in the bitter cold and break the ice until someone did the job and brightened the borough once again.

Andrew Stewart converted a barn into the Ohiopyle House in 1871 just as the B&O opened its line there. Stewart was a man of great vision. Although he retired from Congress in 1850, he was involved in all the major issues of the country in that day. He led the fight to bring this great railway through his Falls City, foreseeing the first tourist boom and allowing his neighbors to prosper along with his own family.

For half a century the Ferncliff Hotel reigned supreme as the entertainment center of the Youghiogheny River Gorge. In 1879, Stewart's sons sold their Fayette Springs Hotel (the Stone House) on the National Road as business fell off with the encroachment of the railroad into this area. The Stewarts built the Ferncliff Hotel and Park above the Ohiopyle Falls, allowing travelers to enjoy the water in grand style.

On the B&O just west of Ohiopyle, unknown folks pose on the double tracks dressed in their Sunday best.

Glotfelty's store sat at the mouth of the steel bridge and next to the B&O tracks in Ohiopyle. This Fourth of July celebration has flags blowing in the breeze. Today in Ohiopyle on Independence Day, folks are not dressed quite so elaborately. The bridge has been replaced. It could not accommodate the millions of visitors who continue to play in the Youghiogheny River Gorge.

I have not been able to acquire much information on this particular Union Supply Store. It obviously sat along the tracks here, was a large building, and was frequented by locals.

Mining was a big business here and throughout neighboring counties. Jake Taylor, Springer Holland (the boss), and Edward Boland pose for the camera after a hard day's work in 1917. The mine rested above Cucumber Falls. Although hundreds of thousands of dollars have been poured into its prevention, during extreme high water, acid mine drainage seeps into Cucumber Run.

There were sawmills on every knob and hillside in these mountains during the great boom. Unknown workers take a break for the camera on the railroad tracks.

Growing up in Ohiopyle can be a wonderful thing, and Roberta Corristan takes advantage of her situation here in 1941. Jim Hochstetler's store sat across the road from the falls until the 1960s, when the state park came here and Route 381 was rerouted. Roberta enjoys a popular Ohiopyle pastime; few pass through our paradise without an ice cream from one of our many parlors.

BATHING ALONG RIVER FRONT, OHIO PYLE, PA.

Even though folks wore modest swimsuits long ago, the fun was the same as it is now. That cool Youghiogheny water keeps us all happy during hot summer days. This scene is above the falls. The Western Maryland Bridge in the background now sits quietly awaiting its refurbishment as part of the Yough Bike/Hike Trail.

The river at Ferncliff Park is pictured here in 1917. Parasols abound as ladies protect their delicate skin from the sun's rays. Today we wear bikinis and sunscreen. Many things have changed, but the river rocks filled with funseekers probably never will.

This is Ross Bryner's sawmill in 1900. Posing for the camera, from left to right, are Springer Holland, unknown, John Wilburn, Bob Wilburn, and Gig Ainsley.

This Ohiopyle sawmill was believed to be in the Kentuck Mountain area. Timbering kept many men working and families eating in this forested area.

Alvertta Shipley stands to the left in this 1924 photo of Castle Rock. Castle Rock once covered the entire area from the woods, across the road, to this small climbing rock. The immense stone was bored through to build a road when the 1919 Meadow Rutt Bridge was constructed. Even this part of the rock was destroyed recently when the Meadow Run Bridge was replaced.

The Meadow Run Bridge was built in 1919 to replace a small wooden structure that sat closer to the Youghiogheny River. In its day, the double-arched design was very modern. This bridge served the town for decades until the narrow lanes became far too small for the large amount of tourist traffic.

Upstream, this Meadow Run Bridge stands close to the Meadow Run Church. The 1912 scene shows, from left to right, Cecelia Collins, Kathryn Collins, Mildred Potter, and Alice Collins (sitting with the fishing pole).

Ohiopyle's Oddfellows Lodge 499 poses for the photographer.

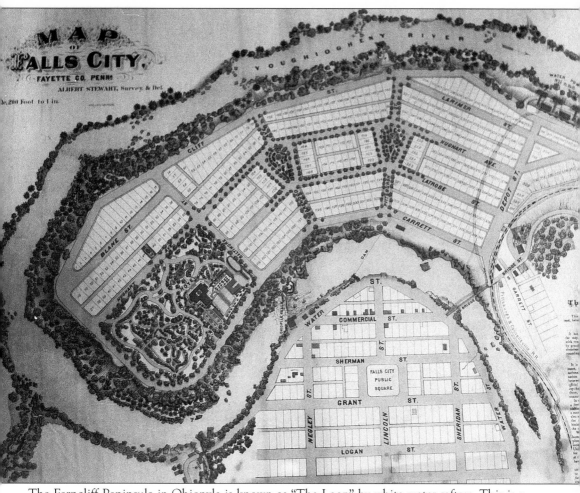

The Ferncliff Peninsula in Ohiopyle is known as "The Loop" by white-water rafters. This is a survey map drawn up by Albert Stewart (son of Andrew) in 1868. Today's Ohiopyle Borough is shown in the area at the bottom. The peninsula here was laid out for a resort town that was never built. The Ferncliff Peninsula has never been developed beyond the Ferncliff Hotel and cabins that are now long gone.

Ross Bryner stands at the "Y" in the road where Route 381 and Dinnerbell Road connect. His farm is in the background. In the 1960s, the state park came to town, fighting locals and taking their land in the name of conservation. Bryner's land is now part of the park.

Clarence Daniels and his dog Butch are seen here in 1946.

Jim Marietta lies on the ground with his dog Rex. From left to right are LeRoy and Tug Morrison, Bob Marietta, and Ralph Morrison. These Ohiopyle fellows are closely related.

This sturdy stone Ohiopyle schoolhouse was built after the wooden one burned down on February 6, 1934. While the new school was being erected, students attended classes in the Ferncliff Hotel and local church basements.

Posing in front of the stone schoolhouse are, from left to right, as follows: (front row) Nellie Lambie, Lois Provance, and Harold Smith; (back row) a Henning boy, Chub Lambi, unknown, and Ray Kurtz.

Tinker Ridge School held classes above Dinner Bell Read just a few miles south of Ohiopyle. In this 1905 photo, the following locals are, from left to right, Charles Collins, Victor Holt, Isiah and William Wable, Nelson and Kathryn Collins, Maude Bryner, Ida Dean, Eugene Collins, Charles Holt, Frank Dean, Clifton Holt, Blanche Bryner, Lena McCartney, and Celia Collins.

Belle Grove School House is shown here in 1915 with teacher Ava King in center. The school was destroyed by a tree that fell on it on August 8, 1936.

These Ohiopyle folks, from left to right, are Hannah and Elasha Bryner, Dick and John Bryner, Noah Holland, and Chester, Calvin, and Jesse Bryner.

This Ohiopyle gathering occurred in the summer of 1899. The two boys in the front with their fiddles are Noah Holland and Charles Bryner. The children in the row behind them are, from left to right, as follows: (middle row) Ethel, Althea, Milton, and Mary Holiday, and Jesse and Chester Bryner; (back row) Billie and Cindy Tressler (holding baby Annabelle), Ross Bryner with his wife, Lucinda Bryner, and their daughter Ada, Richard Bryner, Anna Bryner Holiday, Hiram Holiday, Ella Holland, unknown, Mary and Lida Bryner, Calvin Bryner and his daughter Maude, Hannah Bryner, and Mr. Bryner and his son John.

This is a 1900 photo of Sallie Gilmore Smith rocking on Tom Butler's (later Richard Bryner's) front porch.

This is a September 1902 photo taken at Elasha Bryner's home on Tinker Ridge just south of Ohiopyle. From left to right are Mollie Myers, Mary Lucinda, Sylvania, Ross, and Wesley (in lap), Maude, Jesse, and Chester Bryner, Willie Hall, and Edward Largent.

1917

Hannah and Elasha Bryner of Tinker Ridge, Ohiopyle, are pictured here in 1917.

This 1912 scene shows the triple-arched stone bridge at Indian Creek Valley. The first bridge crossing the creek here was destroyed in a train wreck in 1885. It was replaced with a double-track iron structure which served until this three-arched stone bridge with retaining walls was built in 1900. This was a water station at the time of the photo. Andrew Stewart's son, Col. Andrew Stewart, built a large sawmill nearby and named the tiny village that formed around it Stewarton. Early rafting trips from Ohiopyle were taken out in Stewarton.

The Indian Creek Station in 1933 was still in good repair as the Depression wreaked havoc on the local economy.

Locals came out to pose for this 1890 photograph at the Dunbar Station. Notice the sidling track to the right where coal and timber were hauled to the station.

Bridge Number 300 crossed the Youghiogheny River at the mouth of Dunbar Creek. On the east side of the wooden arch truss structure was Gibson; Wheeler was to the west. The arched braces were not part of the original design but were added later for more support.

This picture of Bridge Number 305 shows a man standing on the short plain bridge at Dunbar in 1890. There was never a shortage of stone to build supports in this neck of the woods.

The first Uniontown Station was quite decorative, as shown in this 1890 photograph. Uniontown is the Fayette County seat. During this time, over two dozen millionaires—all steel, coal, and coke barons—resided here in their palatial mansions. The National Road brought great commerce here during the early and mid-1800s before the railroad and its iron horses became the transportation of choice.

This 1890 scene at the Uniontown Station shows men and boys who seem to be having a leisurely day in their hats and knickers.

This station replaced the old one in 1905 and was in use for over 70 years. The building also served as a train order center until 1913 with the call letters "UD." In 1913, the "FY" tower began operation just 2 miles to the east in Leith.

A man poses down the track on this Uniontown bridge.

This is another Uniontown bridge scene.

The West Penn Line outside of Uniontown is seen here in 1896.

This is another Uniontown West Penn scene from 1896.

The Fayette County Court House on the National Road in Uniontown is the subject of this 1896 photo. The ornate sandstone walls of justice were built in 1891. The building's Henry Hobson-Richardsonian-Romanesque architecture includes a 188-foot clock tower. This job was completed by Laughead, Modisette and Company of Uniontown from blueprints by Pittsburgers Edward M. Butz and William Kaufman.

A bustling Main Street (the National Road) in Uniontown is here in 1896.

This is a view of North Main Street in Uniontown in 1896.

A figure leans on a lamppost on Main Street in Uniontown in 1896.

This 1896 picture depicts trolley service on Main Street. This town was a busy one with many shops and restaurants during this prosperous time.

This 1896 view is of Main Street looking west in Uniontown.

A damsel is in distress is shown in this view of West Fayette Street looking west in 1896.

Mabel at the Fountain stood proudly at the intersection of Morgantown, Church, and South Streets. She was 14 feet high, weighed 3,500 pounds, and served water to humans, horses, and dogs alike. The statue was constructed by J.W. Fist of York, Pennsylvania, and dedicated on July 4, 1896, as a gift from the YMCA and the Women's Christian Temperance Union at the town's centennial celebration.

South Mount Vernon Avenue in Uniontown is pictured here in 1896.

Every town had at least one brewery a hundred years ago, and Uniontown was no different; Uniontown's Fayette Brewing Company is seen here in 1896. Today, such a small establishment would be referred to as a micro-brewery.

The Seamans' home and gardens are pictured here on September 14, 1911.

J.V. Thompson's Oak Hill Estates is the subject of this 1896 photo.

This is Clyde Johnson's grocery store in Uniontown, *c.* 1900.

The Colonial Coke Company Mine Number 2 is here with Clyde Smith on the right. Fayette County and the surrounding region was filled with coal and coke companies while our coal was of the highest quality.

Here is a bird's-eye view of Uniontown looking south in 1896.

This bird's-eye view of Uniontown, in 1986, looks westward.

Shady Grove was once a swimming lake and amusement park/picnic area as can be seen in this turn-of-the-century depiction. Today, the park still reigns as Uniontown's most popular swimming pool.

This picture depicts a Fort Necessity Sunday service in the 1950s.

The Summit Hotel is seen in this May 22, 1912 picture. During the Summit Mountain Hill Climbs and the Uniontown Speedway Boardtrack's racing days, from 1913 to 1922, the Summit Hotel was the center of entertainment. This grand hotel is still in operation today and overlooks Uniontown along the summit on the National Road.

The Third Annual Summit Mountain Hill Climb of 1915 brought 4,000 spectators who lined the sides of the roads and even climbed the mountainsides and telephone poles to get better seats.